FINISHER

YOUR GUIDE TO FINALLY GETTING IT DONE

LaTrice Ryan

Ryan Enterprises
PO BOX 4393
Cordova, TN 38018

Limits of Liability and Disclaimer of Warranty

The author and publisher shall not be liable for your misuse of this material. This book is strictly for informational and educational purposes.

Warning- Disclaimer

The purpose of this book is to inform and educate. The author and/or publisher do not guarantee that anyone following these techniques, suggestions, tips, tools, or strategies will become successful. The author and/or publisher shall have neither liability nor responsibility to anyone with respect to any loss or damage caused, or alleged to be caused, directly or indirectly,
by the information contained in this book.

TABLE OF CONTENTS

ABOUT THE AUTHOR

L aTrice Ryan is the C.E.O. and founder of LaTrice Ryan Ministries. Her ministry is designed to enhance individuals by delivering quality resources: spiritual, psychological, educational, financial, and physiological, which will improve the daily lives of individuals and their family members. With humility and generosity of spirit, LaTrice captivates the minds and hearts of God's people and helps them lead productive purposeful lives.

Her passion for God has led to an anointing to preach and teach the word of God with authority, revelation, and deliverance. Her insightful messages include sobering truths that challenge men and women to pray and cultivate their God-given potential in their personal, spiritual, and professional lives.

LaTrice is a wife and mother who possesses an uncanny ability to reach people of all ages and from various walks of life. She strives to positively influence the lives of God's people through the application of the Word. She continues to build a legacy by writing this book for you. As you read, you can't help but to feel the passion she has for God's people. Take time not only to read the book but apply its principles.

Here's to finishing!

DEDICATION

Thank You, JESUS!! For real, Lord I know I bugged you day and night while writing this book. There were so many times I did not think I could do it, and each time you proved me wrong. Thank you for being EVERYTHING to me. Lord Jesus without You, I am nothing.

To the butter on my popcorn, the sugar in my kool-aid, the cherry to my hot fudge sundae, my baby daddy, my big daddy, and my boyfriend for life, I LOVE ME SOME DEREK RYAN. Derek, thank you for believing in me. I apologize for waking you up in the middle of the night when I would get out of bed to write. I tried to be quiet. It didn't always work. Thank you for being patient with me.

To the pieces of my heart who call me Mama and Honey- I love each of you with every fiber of my being. I honestly cannot wait for you all to read this book.

Thank you to my family for always supporting me. LaTrice Ryan Ministries Staff thank you for building the kingdom with me, you all make ministry easy.

3

Krystal, thank you for listening when I needed to vent and for making me laugh when I wanted to cry. You will always be my little Bird. *Now the world knows your nickname is Bird.*

Mama, thank you for giving me life and for never telling me what I could not do. You have always been my biggest cheerleader, my loudest AMEN; you always told me I was brilliant, beautiful, and bold. Mama, because of you I knew no fear.

Madear, I wish you could have lived to read this. I hope I make you proud.

INTRODUCTION

Since I've been writing this book, I started off with the title "Secure the BAG: Pursuing God's Blessing, Anointing, and Glory." but as I kept writing, God revealed more about me. He showed me the *"Securing* the BAG" Awakening Prayer Call was the inspiration to begin writing, but there was a more personal revelation that would be discovered.

I have been writing a book for 10 years. I would start, then Life happened, and I stopped. I downloaded book writing software. I watched book writing webinars. I even went to the bookstore to look at other books, hoping it would motivate me to write. I would start, not have any inspiration, and stop.

Allow me to be completely honest; I don't do anything I'm not good at nor do I do anything that doesn't push me. Whatever I do, it's because I like doing it and or because it comes naturally to me. I only stretch myself in areas I like. I didn't go to college after high school because I did not want to write research papers. *I have NEVER WRITTEN A TERM PAPER in my life*. I am good at verbally conveying a thought. I am a kinesthetic learner. I am hands on and physical. I learn by doing. I have the willpower to accomplish physical things. Nothing mental.

I type like a tap dancing chicken. I vaguely remember the rules to correct subject-verb agreement. I made every excuse not to write this book and most of my excuses were legitimate. I wouldn't write because I had not renewed my Microsoft 2016 subscription. I wouldn't write because I did not have enough storage in my Dropbox.

Then something internal happened to me on 1/2/18. I remember it so clearly. I had finished the first The Awakening Prayer Call of the year. I was sitting in complete silence, which is what I normally do after prayer. I sit in total silence and listen. I'm not listening to anything. I am listening for something. I wait to hear confirmation, revelation, and affirmation from God. I listen for the smallest, most subtle piece of our massive immeasurable God.

Prayer is two-way communication. I approach prayer as if I am having a conversation with someone I simply cannot live without. Effective communication or in this case prayer involves listening actively and attentively. When we pray God is actively involved in our conversation, once we have said our piece and emptied out our soul, that doesn't end the conversation. As I sat in silence listening and anticipating his response, something extraordinary happened. I heard a Voice that was so loud, yet quiet. The Voice was so loud until my entire body, mind, and spirit followed the leading of This Voice. I don't know how the Voice sounded. I don't know if it was my voice or someone else's voice, but I heard it. Although I never really heard the voice, everything in me did. I started moving towards the thing I put off for the longest of time. I sat at my desk, opened my laptop, clicked on the Microsoft office icon, and attempted to open Microsoft office. I knew what would happen and it happened. "Your Microsoft Office subscription is expired. Please click here to renew." What happened next was unexpected. I did not do what I would normally do. This time I did something different.

Albert Einstein is credited for saying this quote, "Insanity: doing the same thing over and over again and expecting different results." Before I read Einstein's quote, my grandmother once said to me, *Treecee you can't eat a whole pan of cornbread and wonder why you ain't losing weight.* Einstein and Madear were both saying the same thing. If you want

7

something to change, do something different. That is exactly what I did. I renewed the Microsoft subscription, added more storage to Dropbox, and started doing something that I knew would challenge me in an uncomfortable way. Challenges were no stranger to me; I don't want to be challenged AND uncomfortable. Truthfully, if something challenges you but does not make you uncomfortable, your full potential will remain undiscovered. Moreover, when you are challenged and uncomfortable, your faith becomes STRONGER. The ability to trust God in an area that you cannot control builds your faith!

You can't walk by faith on familiar roads!

I started writing. Whoa, I was writing. Man, I was writing. I could not believe where the revelation was coming from. The more I wrote, the more I was able to write. The more I wrote, the more I wanted to write. The more I wrote, the more ideas came, the more inspiration came. The words I was writing had become personal. While I wrote, I saw my vulnerabilities. As I wrote, I had to challenge my comfortability.

I had to face the fact that I had become ***complacent*** in my ministry, career, and in life. Complacency is like a deadly virus dormant in your system ready to kill your goals and dreams. It has the power to rob you blind of new experience, positive change, and personal growth. The worst thing about complacency is that the infected person is usually unaware that he or she is at risk because they feel no pain. When we are complacent, we no longer think strategically about the future. We become too comfortable with our past and current successes. Our thinking becomes short-term, inward, and narrow in focus. When we become so enamored with our past performances or victories that we fail to see new threats coming our way? That probably means you have just purchased a one-way ticket to your comfort zone.

COMPLACENCY WILL LEAD TO EXTINCTION!

"Rustout is the slow death that follows when we stop making the choices that keep life alive. It's the feeling of numbness that comes from taking the safe way, never accepting new challenges, continually surrendering to the day-to-day routine. Rustout means we are no longer growing, but at best, are simply maintaining. It implies that we have traded the sensation of life for the security of a paycheck ... Rustout is the opposite of burnout. Burnout is overdoing ... rustout is underbeing." RICHARD LEIDER and STEVE BUCHHOLTZ, The Rustout Syndrome

In this day and age, we are so overloaded with choice and opportunity that you might even say that we are spoiled for choice. There is just so much that we could do that we often end up not doing anything at all. The abundance that modern life offers us tends to overwhelm us which leads to an emotional overload that will distract you and scatter your effort and concentration. There simply isn't enough time to do everything, but there is always enough time for the most important things in your life. Success at anything in life, whether it be financially, relationally, or physically requires an investment of time and effort from you. It is time to sell your home on complacency avenue and leave the city called Comfort Zone FOR GOOD!

One of the most effective ways to becoming a finisher is to learn and utilize the power of **URGENCY**. What can you do immediately? What action can you take right now that will move you closer to finishing what you've started? I realize there are things in our lives that we want to do that we can't just do RIGHT NOW at the drop of the hat. Like retire, or travel around the world, or buy the dream house. But if these are things you want, you can start working toward them right now.

Make the plan, start to save, ask yourself what you need to do to make it happen. It's never too late to be who you're meant to be. This book is all about ACTION.

Taking the first step, even if it is small will create momentum, and you will almost automatically be driven to take another step. Don't wait for everything to be perfect before you take the first step. Just do it. Just get it going. Often you will only know what to do next after taking that first step.

Here is the question I asked myself prior to abandoning procrastination, complacency, and finally deciding to finish IT: "What is the difference this time?" I still have the same life issues. I still have a demanding itinerant ministry schedule. There are still only 24 hours in a day. I even have three grandchildren now. Ten years ago, I was in my thirties; now I am in my forties. The difference is not having more time, more money, nor more help. The difference is this: I FINALLY realized that I wasted over ten years avoiding something that could have been done in ten seconds. I FINALLY realized had I started over ten years ago, I would have been finished by now. I FINALLY realized that life goes on even when I don't. I heard motivational guru Les Brown say, "It's a shame to die at

25 years old and not be buried until you are 85 years old." I FINALLY realized that even if I am not the best at something, the least, I can do it FINISH IT.

How many God-inspired dreams have you placed on the shelf of procrastination? How much longer will we continue to expect a change without having a plan to bring about change? How many times have you started something just to lose your inspiration mid-stream? How do you keep going when quitting is so much easier? How do you stay positive when you are frustrated? Are you tired of talking yourself out of what God told you to do? Are you ready to FINALLY FINISH IT?

No matter what your IT is:

- Starting a new business
- Finishing your degree
- Finishing a 5K or a marathon
- Maybe you are like me, and you are finishing a book.

If you are ready to advance from being a *Habitual Starter* to a **FINISHER,** grab your pen, highlighter, and notepad because today history is being made. You are putting a plan into action. Today is the day that you ***FINALLY FINISH IT!***

Chapter 1

SET THE TARGET

There are already millions of words written about the setting and achieving of your goal, which are practiced by millions of people as well. But still, most of the goals created are not fulfilled. Every New Year, the health and fitness industry experience a boost in gym memberships. For the first few weeks of the new year, the parking spaces are few, there's a wait to use the treadmills, and the aerobics classes are full. However, by the first week of March (sometimes sooner than that) the New Year's rush is over. The weight loss goal is not met. Clean eating is replaced with ordering a Venti Double Carmel Macchiato with extra whip cream. The issue was NOT creating the goal; the issue was not having a clear path on how to achieve the goal.

What is Your Why?

It's very easy to say you're going to accomplish something, anything, in the next 12 months. You can say you're going to be 20 pounds lighter or you'll be living in a new city after a year or you can even say you're going to find the love of your life soon and tie the knot in the next 12 months!

You can do a lot of things, be in a lot of places and meet loads of new people in under a year. You have an infinite number of possible goals you can choose to achieve. Your chosen goal could be in response to a challenge from your friends or maybe a personal challenge you want to take on. No matter the reason behind your desire to succeed at something new, you need one very important skill to achieve that goal.

Can you guess what that skill is? It's self-discipline, of course! Committing to a long-term goal is the beginning of your journey. Once you've done a mental handshake with yourself or signed on an imaginary dotted line confirming your commitment to a specific goal, then your desire to accomplish your goal should kick into high gear.

You need to lock yourself in and buckle up, so you don't get left behind to reach your goal. You need the stamina and the strength to surpass and overcome all obstacles in order to meet your goal.

Before you can begin, you need to know the answer to the question, "What is your why?" What do you hope to achieve with your goal? What's your end game? If you don't know the answer to this question, you need to seriously rethink your goal.

Is it even feasible? Is it something you can possibly hope to do within the timeframe you've given yourself? If you've assessed your goal correctly and you've done the mental gymnastics to confirm it is indeed feasible for you, then congratulations. You've done a great job with the first step!

If you think you made a mistake setting the goal and you don't think it's feasible at all, you're welcome to back out or cross it out of your list and replace it with a more realistic goal. There's no need to push yourself into doing something that's highly improbable or even impossible for you to achieve. Some people may say nothing is impossible. But I beg to disagree. According to Luke 1:37, "For with God nothing will be impossible." The key word is, WITH GOD, nothing is impossible. When we attempt tasks, goals, or projects that are totally outside the will of GOD, we will run into boatloads of obstacles and challenges. We are not created equal. We all know for a fact that some people have more financial resources than others. Some folks are just really blessed to not have to work hard for something that other people need to work their fingers off for! When I was in high school, I did not want to take physical education, so I chose to enroll in JROTC (Junior Reserved Officer Training Corps). This is where my love for the military was sparked. Some cadets struggled with land navigation exercises. Some cadets struggled with various drill exercises. Not me, I was naturally good at being a then cadet, better at being a soldier in the US Army, and now even better at being a soldier in the Army of The Lord. You may have colleagues who are favored ones, the exceptions to the rule. There are things you are naturally good at, and there are those things that you are not naturally good at doing. Just be realistic in your goal setting. That's all!

Here are some important tips that will help you finish the goals that you have.

1) Your goals should be original.

This doesn't mean that such goals need not to be somehow similar or same as the other goals of other individuals. It just means that you should have your own goal, not a second hand one. Many people are practicing to have their goals based on the expectation and hopes of their cultural norms, society, parents, and teachers. This results to cases that wherein you cannot hold such goals for long periods of times. *Disclaimer: You may notice that I refer to losing weight or "Fighting the Jiggling Devil"; as I often refer to my journey of losing weight; pretty often.* Reason being that is the area in my life that I set the most goals most often. I've hired trainers. I've held memberships in just about every gym in my area. I've watched or downloaded workout videos From Billy Banks' Tae-Bo to P90X. Fad diets from Low Carb to the Cabbage Soup diet; from low calorie to the Metabolic Diet, I have tried. I did not achieve any progress in *"Fighting the Jiggling Devil"* until I realized the goal of the diet, trainer, or exercise video would not be achieved until the ultimate goal becomes a priority in my life. Remember that setting a goal truly means that you should earn fulfilment and happiness as you accomplish it

Practice setting goals that are originally yours, not that assumed or inherited. If it is not just from you, what will be the meaning of it? Accomplishing them will not give you that happiness and fulfilment in life.

2) Your goals should be inspirational.

17

Inspiration is something that you feel on the inside. Inspiration is internal. Motivation is something from the outside that compels you to take action. Motivation is external. Inspiration is a driving force, while motivation is a pulling force. Your passion must represent the kind of goals that you have. It should not be any promise or simply wants that you want. It must be something that will drive you to strive harder and be fulfilled in the end as you obtained it.

Passion is that something which pushes you to do whatever it takes to have your goals. It keeps you on the track. It strengthens your concentration and motivates you. It is the passion that inspires you and leads you to the right way going to your desired goal. We will discuss the importance of passion in greater detail later on in the book. KEEP READING.

3) Your goals should be in synch with you spiritually, emotionally, mentally, and even physically.

All your goals must be according to your perspectives and dreams in life. They must not contradict one another.

In January 2015, I fired my job yes you read that right; I fired my secular job to enter into full-time ministry and to build Ryan

Enterprises. At that point, I had been in ministry for fifteen years. Before me firing my job, I juggled working full time, being a wife and mother, plus preaching and traveling. I had goals as a wife, a mom, in my career, and goals in ministry. As our ministry began to grow and expand, we were making a significant impact in our community. We launched several initiatives that required a lot of my attention. My itinerant preaching schedule was increasing. I was preaching locally or regionally every weekend. Not to mention I am a mom to a beautifully blended family of seven children including a young son. WHEW! My goals begin to contradict; more like crash and burn with one another. I needed the financial security of my career while at the same time the Kingdom needed me. I needed to be in total synchrony with my goals. It's almost like driving a car that needs a wheel alignment. When the wheels of the car are not aligned, there is uneven pressure on the tires. They tend to push against each other. When that happens, the car faces uneven friction and much more resistance from the road surface. It results in the tire becoming bald on one side. A bad wheel alignment can also be dangerous because it may cause your car to pull or drift out of your lane or hydroplane on wet pavement. And, uneven tire wear can lead to a blowout or make you lose traction in an emergency. When our goals contradict, we run the risk of a BLOWOUT. In my case, my career was causing my life to be out of divine alignment. By all means, I am not suggesting that you "Fire your job" tomorrow. It took me FIFTEEN YEARS to get to the place of now working full time in ministry. Now that I am working for the *"Greatest Boss in the Universe"* (Jesus), my goals STILL have to be in synch with one another.

4) The goals of you must be realistic in nature. Set a goal you can actually achieve. In 2016, I set a goal to lose forty pounds by my fortieth birthday. I gave myself one year to lose the weight. Could I have lost the weight sooner? Possibly, but did I? NO! I never lost the forty pounds because it was an unrealistic goal for my body type and metabolism. Losing forty pounds by my fortieth birthday was a catchy hashtag, but it was unrealistic for me. On the contrary, I did achieve a realistic goal. I lost weight, inches, I gained muscle tone and improved my overall fitness level. I felt an overwhelming sense of accomplishment, and I looked good in my birthday dress. WINNING!!

Realistic goal doesn't mean that you must have the usual goal of everybody. There are goals sometimes which seem unachievable for everybody, but determined people were able to do so, such as finishing a marathon, building a computer, or inventing an airplane. These goals are attainable and do not let anybody set a limit for you. Mary Kay Ash, the founder of Mary Kay cosmetics, says, "Aerodynamically, the bumblebee shouldn't be able to fly, but the bumblebee doesn't know it, so it goes on flying anyway."

5) Make your goals specific.

You must have a specific goal in order for you to be able to do the right attack towards it. This is not the place to have vague, unspecified or ambiguous goals. Ambiguous goals produce ambiguous results. Your goals should be as detailed as possible. Otherwise, they won't give you enough direction to follow through. According to the American Psychological Association, setting specific goals led to a higher performance 90 percent of the time for companies studied. Goals are like a lamp lighting the way-- the brighter the light, the clearer the road ahead. PROVERBS 29:18 AMP "Where there is no vision [no revelation of God and His word], the people are unrestrained; But happy and blessed is he who keeps the law [of God]."

To make sure your goal sticks in your mind, to make it appear real, you need to make your goal as specific as possible. Don't just say you want to lose weight. For women, you can say something along these lines.

- Keep your goal simple- if it's too complex it means you probably won't do it.
- Keep your goal sensible- if it doesn't make sense, you probably won't do it.
- Keep your goal significant- if you don't value it, you probably won't do it.

Here is an example:

"I'll walk 30 minutes every other day, drink at least 5 glasses of water a day and stop drinking soda in order to lose 10 pounds in 2 months."

6) Your goals should be flexible.

Several people miss the chances of gaining their goals because their concentration with those goals is too extreme and constricted to recognize better goals as they go.

Ensure that you will concentrate on achieving your goal and not with the method or ways on how you can have it. If you find yourself in a rut but feel like you're working hard towards your goal, step back and assess exactly what you are following through with. Are you following through with the plan or with the goal? The plan might be outdated or just wrong, to begin with. If you are truly following through with your goals, you may need to continue with your existing plan, mix it up or take a break. Be flexible enough to choose your best option.

7) You must visualize the process of obtaining your goals.

Faith is visualizing the future. It's believing it before you see it. Hebrews 11:1 says, "Faith is the confidence that what we hope for will actually happen; it gives us assurance about things we cannot see" (NLT, second edition). A lot of people say, "I'll believe it when I see it!" God says the exact opposite is true: "You will see it when you first believe it." There are many things in life that have to be believed before they can be seen. Visualizing your goals in life will help you a lot and will serve as your motivation through the way. Imagining them makes them more realistic and believable, thus ending up in energizing you and inspiring you to strive harder in finishing them.

8) SPEAK, SPEAK, and REPEAT your goals.

You must believe in yourself that the goal that you have is doable. Keep it in your mind that if you will not believe in your goal, then you can never have it. If you will not have a passion for it, then you can never attain success. You must be that someone to speak about your goal. Proverbs 18:21 NIV says, "The tongue has the power of life and death, and those who love it will eat its fruit." Affirm your goals daily, or as often as you need to. Say them aloud. It is one thing to write them down only. We must write the goals and recite our goals.

9) Have a timely set of goals.

It is in time and space where everything exists. Set a specific period of time for the goals to become true or you spend lots of your time in achieving only one and will never have any fulfilment at all. We are interrupted nearly every three minutes, according to Gloria Mark, professor of informatics at University of California, Irvine. What is even more shocking than that is half those interruptions are self-imposed. When you're working on something without a clear deadline, seeing it through to its end can be a huge challenge. Remember the home improvement project you started? One wall of the room is Electric Purple while the other three are eggshell white. Think of all the books you've started but never finished. Of course, you will finish this book. Without setting a deadline to complete a goal, the goal never fully becomes a goal; it remains a wish.

10) Make a list of all the goals that you want to finish.

It has been proven through studies that people who jot down their goals have higher ability of accomplishing their tasks rather than those who only list such goals in their minds. People who don't have a list of their goals are more likely to withdraw from the achievement process.

But still, there are some individuals who manage to set and achieve their goals successfully, even without writing them down. Do not pretend that you are one of those. It is much better to write them down since it is not guaranteed that you are still going to remember all the goals that you have after a long period of time. This is especially true for those of us who are 2 Corinthians 5:7 Faith Walkers "For we walk by faith, not by sight." There are so many visions, goals, dreams, ideas, bottled up in our spirit. That's great. However, a law is not legal until it is written and recorded in government. Habakkuk 2:2

"Then the Lord answered me and said, Write the vision and engrave it plainly on [clay] tablets So that the one who reads it will run."

Why does writing down your goals and dreams have such a profound impact? The explanation has to do with the way our brains work. As you may know, your brain has a left and a right hemisphere. The right side of the brain is your creative, imaginative center. The right side of your brain allows you to dream in color. This side of the brain can take a blank canvas and create a masterpiece. The left hemisphere of the brain is more analytical. The left side of the brain uses logic, facts, and data. Most left side brain dominant individuals do not necessarily dream in color; they are more black and white.

If you just THINK about one of your goals or dreams, you're only using the right hemisphere of your brain, which is your imaginative center. But, if you think about something that you desire, and then write it down, you also tap into the power of your logic-based left hemisphere. And you send your mind and every cell of your body a signal that says, "I want this, and I mean it!" Just the act of writing down your dreams and goals ignites an entirely new dimension of insight, ideas, and productivity to the powerhouse that is your mind.

Be Accountable to Yourself

If you practice self-accountability, you develop a sense of ethics. You don't lie to yourself; you don't deliberately take shortcuts which could eventually backfire. In short, you are honest with yourself, and you take responsibility for your actions. This is very important when building self-discipline because it keeps you in line, it keeps you in check, and it keeps you contained, so you don't go beyond the narrow path you've set for yourself. If you do something that's detrimental to your goal, you acknowledge it. You don't hide it; you don't attempt to write it off. Instead, you face it, and you promise yourself you won't do it again. And you continue on your path to fulfilling your goal, all the while keeping your actions in line with your goal.

So how do you keep yourself accountable? Most experts suggest keeping a journal to write your thoughts and daily experiences in. You can use an old-fashioned piece of paper (smile), or you can just use a tablet or computer. Whatever you choose to write on, make sure you actually put it to good use.

That means, WRITE on it. What do you write down? Write down everything you do from the time you wake up to just before you go to sleep. All your experiences for the day, your adventures, anything that's a mini-step to reaching your goal. Write down your tasks and accomplishments at work, any new stuff you've learned, what you did well and what you could improve on.

You could also write down your negative thoughts and any doubts or fears you may have about your goal. You could then write down your responses to your fears. Doing this is helpful and calls out the fear. Just look up your positive answers, and it should hopefully bring you out of your funk.

Are you spending enough time working on achieving your goal or are you wasting it on watching TV or lying in bed doing nothing? Remember, you're accountable to yourself. So, if you're procrastinating, you're not doing something good. You need to stop such behavior and focus on doing positive actions that will help you reach your goal.

CHAPTER 2

PROCRASTINATING – STOP IT!

Overthinking doesn't sound so bad on the surface-- thinking is good, right? But overthinking can cause problems and procrastination. When you overthink, your judgments get cloudy, and your stress gets elevated. You spend too much time in the negative. Overthinking will cause you to talk yourself out of following your dreams. In many cases, overthinking is caused by a single emotion: fear. When you focus on all the negative things that might happen, it's easy to become paralyzed. The Apostle Paul writes, "Finally, brethren, whatever things are true, whatever things are noble, whatever things are just, whatever things are pure, whatever things are lovely, whatever things are of good report, if there is any virtue and if there is anything praiseworthy—meditate on these things." Philippians 4:8 (NKJV)

I often use this illustration in my sermons. "When you are watching television, if what you are watching is violent, disturbing, or simply boring. You don't continue watching something that you don't like. You grab your remote control and change the channel. Just because it's on television does not mean you have to watch it." Next time you sense that you are starting to spiral in that overthinking direction, grab the spiritual remote control in your life and change the channel. Visualize all the things that can go right and keep those thoughts present and up front.

Here are LaTrice's Three P's to Prevent Overthinking:

Put it in perspective- It's always easy to make things bigger and more negative than they need to be. The next time you catch yourself making a mountain out of a molehill, ask yourself how much it will matter in five years. Or, for that matter, next month. Just this simple question, changing up the time frame, can help shut down overthinking.

Progress over Perfection- This is a big one. For all of us who are waiting for perfection, we can stop waiting right now. Being ambitious is great but aiming for perfection is unrealistic, impractical, and debilitating. The moment you start thinking "This needs to be perfect" is the moment you need to remind yourself, "Waiting for perfect is never as smart as making progress."

Put your best foot forward- The fear that grounds overthinking is often based on feeling that you aren't good enough--not smart enough or hardworking enough or dedicated enough. Once you've given an effort your best, accept it as such and know that, while success may depend in part on some things you can't control, you've done what you could do.

You can't have a regretful thought and a grateful thought at the same time, so why not spend the time being grateful? My grandmother used to say, "Some of us would complain about being hungry while carrying a loaf of bread." Every morning and every evening, make a list of what you are grateful for. Overthinking is something that can happen to anyone. But if you remember *LaTrice's Three P's to Prevent Overthinking* dealing with it you can at least ward off some of the negative, anxious, stressful thinking and turn it into something useful, productive, and efficient.

Good & Bad Habits

Establishing good habits will help you with over thinking because it becomes second nature. Being productive and efficient starts with habits to success. Habits are actions or behavior patterns that you do out of rote, out of repetition. It's become so ingrained in your daily life, and you've become so used to it that you start doing it involuntarily. You don't even need to think about doing your habit before you do it, you just do.

There are two types of habits. Good habits and bad habits. If you want to master self-discipline, you have to let go of your bad habits and replace them with new, positive ones. Bad habits are negative behavior patterns that are a hindrance or a roadblock to your mental and physical health, including any goals you've set for yourself. Laziness, unhealthy eating habits, rude behavior, bullying, swearing, and procrastination are examples of bad habits that really does nothing for you and does not contribute to your growth.

Of course, saying goodbye to a bad habit is easier said than done and is practically impossible to do overnight. It's called a habit because you do it involuntarily, so it's going to take a lot of self-conscious effort on your part to stop doing your bad habits.

Some experts say it will take a minimum of 3 weeks to a month for a person to totally forego his bad habits. It will take plenty of mental and physical effort to do this, but in the end, you'll be better off without your bad habits weighing you down.

So how do you replace a bad habit with a good habit? Good habits come in many different forms. There are simple habits, and there are physically demanding habits which might be difficult to master at first.

Assuming you're also working on breaking your bad habits, it would be best to start with a simple and easy-to-implement habit. After all, you don't want to overwhelm yourself and get stressed with the thought of doing too much at once. When overwhelmed, some people tend to procrastinate so working on too many habits at once may just backfire on you.

To narrow down some good habits you should pick up on, write down a list of habits you would like to acquire. If you really, really want to pick up an exciting but complicated habit, you can break it down into smaller bite-sized habits. Remember, it's easier to implement simple habits than highly complicated ones. Once you've written your proposed habits, write a score beside each habit and choose the one that came out easiest based on your scoring system.

Work on this habit every day for at least a month. Remember how we talked about journals and how you should be writing down everything you do in a day? Well, make sure this habit-forming activity of yours gets written down too. And don't forget to review your journal every week or so just to see how you're getting along with your progress.

When your new habit has finally become a real habit, it's time to work on the next positive habit you should acquire. Just rinse and repeat this process and try to retain as many positive habits as you can – habits that will help you fulfill your tasks at home, at work, or anywhere else.

Here's why building one good habit at a time is important for self-discipline success:

1. You're taking action. Even just the act of trying to get a new habit will require self-discipline. The more you take action, the more your new habit gets ingrained.

2. Your chances of failure are greatly reduced. Your good habits will be so ingrained in your brain that you do it by rote, without conscious thinking. If you committed the right action to memory, failing would be minimized.

3. It helps you build confidence and momentum. You're training yourself to be confident with one good habit. If you succeed, you'll feel pretty confident, and you'd be encouraged to take on another positive habit.

4. It requires you to be responsible and accountable. Forming a good new habit will help you to become responsible since you've tasked yourself to do it repeatedly.

Here are a few examples of good habits:

1. Get up early in the morning (don't stay in bed until noon).

2. Exercise daily (even if you're busy, find a way to fit it into your schedule).

3. Eat a full breakfast (this is the first meal of the day so don't skip it).

4. Drink plenty of water every day (stop drinking too many soft drinks).

The Morning Manna Routine

Many experts claim the morning ritual routine is one of the most important habits everyone should practice. This is because research has shown that a shocking 90% of successful individuals have a morning ritual habit. CEOs of big companies such as Twitter CEO Jack Dorsey, PepsiCo CEO and high-powered politicians wake up very early in the morning to do their routines before heading off to work.

Let me share with you my Morning Manna Routine.

I generally wake up every morning at 3:45 AM. Before my feet hit the ground, I will lay completely still and take about 20 deep breaths. Next, I visualize finishing the most challenging task of the day. I don't focus on the obstacles it takes to finish the task, I focus on finishing the task altogether. Once I am awake, I get dressed and head to gym. Most ministry leaders receive revelation and downloads from God during their prayer time in their office or study. Not me, God speaks to me when I am running on the treadmill or outside. When I need clarity, insight, revelation, or wisdom, I can hear Jesus speaking to me so clear during my morning run. Breathing, visualizing finishing the job, and exercise is the thing that revs my engines every morning.

Generally speaking, waking up early in the morning when everything's quiet is great for meditating, praying or reading inspiring books and quotes. During this special time, turn off your gadgets and focus on renewing your mind. Write down your thoughts, and plan your entire day. Doing this helps you get your mind and body ready for the day ahead. You can even identify your two most important tasks for the day and try to get it done first thing in the morning so that by afternoon you're free to do less important tasks.

Another significant activity you can squeeze in during your morning ritual is exercising. It clears your head and running on a treadmill for even just 5-10 minutes will reduce stress and help boost your metabolism.

Lastly, another habit successful people do in their morning rituals is they prepare their food for the whole day, right up to dinner. Sure you can eat out from time to time, but it's so much better and healthier to prepare your food at home especially if you're counting calories. Eating out is like a calorie-fest where you get twice, three or even 5 times the normal calories you get from cooking your own food!

For night owls, adapting to this lifestyle and changing habits would probably be tremendously difficult at first. Try adapting slowly. Sleep 15 minutes earlier each night to wake up 15 minutes earlier as well. Do this cycle until you get used to sleeping in early and waking up early too.

Implementing the morning ritual habit is very highly recommended by time management and behavior experts. Yes, it will be difficult, but this is why you work on developing one habit at a time. Do this process slowly over a period of weeks. In a month or so you should see some progress, and you'd then be more productive, and you'll have a clearer path to reaching your goals. Developing positive habits is very important for your success.

What or Who is holding you back?

The biggest obstacle to your goals and your dreams are all in your head. That's right; mental obstacles are your biggest enemy. We have millions of thoughts and ideas swirling in our brain all the time, and not all of them are going to be positive. In fact, many would be downright negative. Here are some perfect examples of negative thoughts that can obstruct your road to success:

- I can't do it. It's too difficult.

- I'm too busy right now. I'll do it later.

- I'm going to fail miserably.

- What will people think of me if I fail?

- What's going to happen if I succeed? My life would change.

- They're all better than me. I'm never going to beat them.

- They don't like me. They're looking at me like I'm going to fail already.

- I quit.

Sound familiar? I'm sure you've had one or all of these negative thoughts running through your head at one time or another. Maybe even now.

So how do you overcome these mental obstacles? I'm not even going to say it's easy because curing something mentally is different from curing a physical ailment. But a good start is by standing tall and believing in yourself. Self-confidence is key to obliterating mental roadblocks. Be firm in your decision and stop doubting yourself. The key takeaway here is if you don't believe in yourself, no one will. That's a fact.

The second obstacle you would have to overcome would be physical obstacles. If during the course of chasing down your dreams, an accident occurs and you're left with a physical injury, then this is an obstacle. But don't despair because plenty of people, including superstar athletes, have fallen and gotten injured but many are still able to rise back up and continue their journey.

The third obstacle lying in your path would be financial obstacles. If your goal involves funding from outside sources or investors, then you need to work hard to get them to trust you and your business model, so they'll invest and spend their money on you. If you don't get a yes from a single investor, don't despair. There are other ways to drum up the cash. If you're determined, passionate and driven to succeed, sooner or later investors are going to come knocking at your door.

The fourth obstacle would be time. Having too much or too little time can both present themselves as obstacles to your success. If you have too much time, you can easily get distracted. If you don't have the self-discipline, you could get bored and do stuff you wouldn't normally do if you were busy. So try to be busy and be productive. It's okay to relax from time to time but not too much. If you have too little time to chase your dreams, then you need to FIND the time. You need to make some room for your dreams. No matter how busy you get, you must find pockets of time which you can devote to working on your dream. I recommended you pick up the morning rituals habit so you can squeeze in some personal time before your day begins. This is the perfect time to work on your goals and your dreams.

The fifth obstacle on our list would be distractions or temptations. If you don't have self-discipline, you'll be fair game for getting distracted easily. Are your friends inviting you to a dinner party? Party versus boring dream? It's a no-brainer, right? Party, here I come! Instead of working on your goals, you're going to go to the party. This would, of course, be the wrong decision. If you're the hanging out – having fun all the time type, you'd need to work doubly hard on your self-discipline so you can resist this particular weakness. If you're able to conquer this, your path to success just got a whole lot clearer.

Let's suppose you planned to be at your computer, working on a project, at 10 a.m. on a Monday morning, but you're not. How come? The answer may be one or more of the following:

- Woke up late.

- Are you too sapped?– the coffee hasn't set in yet.

- Are you overly hyper? – drank too much coffee and can't sit motionlessly.

- Are you distracted by the weather? – love to take a walk or bike ride.

- Are you distracted by the weather? – it's atrocious and depressing.

- Got a telephone call (or e-mail or text message) from a friend, who's depressed (though not in crisis) and asked to talk.

- Got a telephone call from a friend (or e-mail or text message) that's happy and wished to share great news.

- Are you googling ridiculous questions like, "How tall is Jesus?"

- Are you spending endless hours shopping online?

- Are you playing Candy Crush?

- Switched on the television for "a minute" and saw that one of your favorite actors was being interviewed, so you decide to view the interview.

- Simply realized that the same load of laundry has been in the dryer for three days.

These are common things that may throw you off your course. It's only a partial list; naturally, you may likely add many other entries to it. There are likely 100s of potential "bumps" that may knock you off your course.

One crucial thing to point out is that, while a few of these bumps appear "good" or "worthwhile" and some seem "frivolous," they're all equally unacceptable from the viewpoint of beating your procrastination habit.

You'll need to learn to resist the urge to get absorbed into activities not on your schedule, regardless how crucial or virtuous they appear at the moment. The one exception, naturally, is emergencies, by which I mean actions that can't be put off without significant harm to yourself or other people. However even with an emergency, after you've handled it, ask yourself whether it may have been prevented by finer planning, or whether somebody else could have handled it. If you've got a challenging goal, it's really crucial to learn to minimize the number of preventable emergencies in your life and to learn to delegate as much as conceivable.

3 Tips To Follow

1. Always start Your Day with a Schedule

Scheduling is crucial as having no schedule opens the door to the sorts of fears and doubts that may lead to procrastination. Ideally, you'll know how to produce a manageable schedule that reflects your core values. If not, at least come up with an easy schedule that states explicitly what you're going to be doing or working on each hour of the day. Attempt to produce your schedule the night before so that the act of scheduling itself doesn't itself become a sort of procrastination.

2. Be Prepared

The Boy Scouts got this one right. For the same reason as #1, above to prevent confusion that may throw you off your course you have to start your day with all the data, tools, and materials required to achieve your work right out there in front of you. That signifies everything: books, paper files, PC files, phone numbers, writing implements, even paper clips. It ought to all be available, organized and in perfect working order.

3. Don't Make It Harder Than It Is

Don't fall into the trap of presuming that procrastination is inevitable. Popular culture likes to portray the act of production as a sort of epic battle because it makes great drama, but that's the inappropriate model to follow. Rather, you ought to approach your work with a light touch, and the experience ought to be like a play: simple, safe and fun.

CHAPTER 3
STICK WITH IT!!

Achieving even the simplest of goals requires us to learn the meaning of commitment. Throughout our life, we are reminded of commitment, whether it's related to personal or business goals, and we realize that without committing, we can't achieve anything.

When you think about it, everything you ever achieved came from a commitment you made; whether it's your children, your degree, your job, or even your house. Learning how to commit is not simply about making commitments. However, it's about keeping those commitments in the face of foreseen and unforeseen hurdles. Easier said than done, right?

There is a difference between being involved and being committed. My husband would use this riddle to convey a point to our children:

Question: In a bacon and egg breakfast, what's the difference between the chicken and the pig?

Answer: The chicken is involved, but the pig is COMMITTED! When you want your project to succeed, you invest yourself in it fully.

Why? Because you can't afford to only be involved; being involved means you're not committed enough, and if you're not committed enough, that thing you've been working on, will not happen. Many people are attached to comfort, safety, and the easiest way to do it. These values are important, however, to truly grow and expand we must find an area of our life where commitment supersedes comfort.

Commitment is what inspires us to take action. Being committed is a willingness to do whatever it takes to fulfill and follow through on a responsibility. It may not even be what we most enjoy, but nonetheless, being committed means, we are going to do it regardless. Commitment is essential to being a winner and achieving our God-ordained goals.

How do you know if you are committed or involved?

A primary key to knowing we are committed is when we are willing to make a sacrifice in order to achieve our goals. When my husband and I were dating, we were very clear on the type of relationship we wanted. We both were divorced, we both were rebuilding our lives. We both were in ministry. For us, that meant that we were conscious of how to date and how our relationship would be viewed. We wanted our courtship to reflect Jesus and our commitment to the call of ministry. For us, that meant we would be exclusively dating each other. We opted out of the casual dating thing. We decided to date with a purpose. The purpose was MARRIAGE. This style of dating cannot work unless both individuals in the relationship are clear that this is what they BOTH want and they both are ready not just to be involved with each other but to be committed to one another. As we grew on our journey, our relationship evolved. We fell in love. Derek asked me to marry him, and of course, I accepted. We had several goals we set for our marriage, but the main goal is this: NO DO-OVERS. We were and still are committed to making us work. Divorce is not an option for Team Ryan. Ok, we often hear "You can't predict the future, or you don't know what life will bring your way." That is true. To the contrary, you can control what you commit to. You can control what you are willing to sacrifice to achieve a goal. Don't throw away a good thing because you're having a bad moment. Commitment is the resolve to succeed during the good, the bad; during the summer season and the cold winters. Being committed doesn't remove the difficulty, the fear, or any other negative emotion. It means we are willing to give-up the convenient and comfort to get the job done.

To have commitment we must find the meaning and purpose behind the mission we are pursuing. Purpose is similar to passion, and the development of a passion that spurs us toward our mission is half the battle of achieving goals. Passion is what drives us forward. It's what gets us out of bed each day and what keeps us awake with excitement at night. Without an inner sense of purpose and motivation, it becomes much more challenging to sustain commitment. Look deep inside yourself and begin examining what ignites your passion for life right now. Explore this area as an area of commitment.

PASSION

What makes you come alive? What ignites a fire in your soul and really lights you up?

Our passions are what give life its juice. To discover your passion, and follow up on it is one of the better ways you can use your time.

Even if you do know what you genuinely love, many of us feel that it is selfish to spend time and energy on doing things 'just for fun.' We believe we should be serious and responsible, and spend our time working hard at accomplishing goals. We feel worthy and virtuous when we attend to endless tasks and slave away at tasks we detest. We feel ashamed about spending time on things that make us feel alive and happy. What a distorted way of looking at things!

Discovering your life passion can mean the difference between happiness and frustration. Do you know what you are passionate about? Is there anything in your life that makes you feel genuinely good, Excited and alive? If not, either you have not found your life passion yet, or you are disregarding it.

Doing what makes you happy is not frivolous or selfish- it is smart. Being pleased makes you healthier, more productive, and nicer to be around. In addition, whom are you actually helping by working yourself into the ground doing things that do not satisfy you?

Does anybody truly benefit from the fact that you have an alphabetized spice rack, work fifty hours a week, and say 'yes' to so many requests that you have no energy to give to any of them? Do these things make you happy?

If not, it is time to check how you are spending the treasured minutes and hours of your life. When is the last time you spent a couple of hours doing something that made you feel genuinely alive? That made the time fly past, and left you feeling energized instead of ran out?

It may have been a while, but if you actually give it some thought, you will probably come up with something. If you genuinely cannot seem to find your passion, there are a couple of ways you can figure it out.

One way is to experiment. Try some new activities. The only way you will find out what you love doing is by doing it. Who knows, you may discover a passion for organizing closet space, writing poetry, or creating personalized baby onesies.

Next, you need to find small ways to search for your passion and include it in your life. How about making cards for birthdays and other occasions? Try with joining an art class or decorating your personal space. I bet that a beautiful collage above your desk would bring you more joy than perfectly tidy desk drawers.

As you find your passion and more time and ways to activate it, you become happier. This makes others happier too. Who'd you rather see each day at breakfast, somebody bored and frustrated, or somebody filled with enthusiasm? I'll take the latter for $200 Alex.

The creative force behind all great art, all great drama, all great music, all great architecture, all great writing is passion. Nothing great is ever accomplished in life without passion. Nothing great is ever sustained in life without passion. Passion is what energizes life. Passion makes the impossible possible. Passion gives you a reason to get up in the morning and go, "I'm going to do something with my life today." Without passion life becomes boring. It becomes monotonous. It becomes routine. It becomes dull. God created you with the emotions to have passion in your life, and He wants you to live a passionate life. Passion is what mobilizes armies into action. Passion is what causes explorers to boldly go where no man's gone before. Passion is what causes scientists to spend late night hours trying to find the cure for a dreaded disease. Passion is what takes a good athlete and turns him or her into a great athlete where they're breaking records. You've got to have passion in your life.

Romans 12:1 *"Never be lacking in zeal, but keep your spiritual fervor."* Keep the fires going in your life. Circle the word "keep." Notice, it's not automatic. It's a choice. It's a discipline. It's something you must maintain. You are not by nature passionate about God. It's something that you must choose to do.

Passion cannot be found in your head because it lives in your heart. Passion is to your goals what gasoline is to a car. It is the inner element that keeps you going. It is the spark in your heart. When you talk about it everything in you wakes up, your posture straightens up, your eyes are brighter. When you are **happy doing something**, there's a hint of what you are passionate about right there. Passion is engrained in your body and soul. Time seems to fly by when you are doing something you are passionate about. Don't take your passion for granted. Psalm 37:4 says, "Delight yourself in the Lord and He will give you the desires of your heart." This Scripture doesn't just mean that God will give you what you want. It means that He will place within you the desires of your heart - your passion, dreams, and goals. And more importantly, He will use your passion for the purpose of making a difference in the lives of others.

What am I passionate about?

Usually what you are passionate about started when you were a child. For example;

You would go outside and make gourmet mud pies. Your mud pies were made with the finest dirt from your mother's flower bed. You dug up her perfectly bloomed hydrangeas to garnish your mud pies. Your loving for cooking and baking didn't end in your childhood; it carried on to your teenage years. You were a culinary expert with Hamburger Helper and Ramen Noodles. Before you could start your homework, you were in the kitchen learning how to spruce up a basic boxed noodle meal. By the time you finished adding extra seasoning, your own secret sauce the ordinary after-school quick meal was a delicious masterpiece. That passion for cooking didn't end there. Throughout college, your dorm room was better than "Waffle House." Your dorm became known as "The Spot." You had a portable stove, George Foreman Grill, and a mini oven in your room. If the cafeteria was closed, your room was on and popping. You graduated from college with a bachelors of science in basket weaving. Because *somebody* said, "Go to school for basket weaving. You will surely find a job when you graduate college." It turns out *somebody* was right. You landed a job at Basket Weaving Inc. You settle into your new career as Quality Control Inspector of Baskets.

Life is good. You have a career, paying your bills. You are grateful to God for blessing you with the job. After all, countless of job seekers would love to be in your shoes. But something is missing; you are BORED. You've lost your sparkle. You're unfulfilled. You are using your degree, but you are not using your PASSION. Skills can be learned, but your passion is a part of who you are and your natural God-given talent.

An unused talent will cause you to lose your passion for life and your passion for God.

1 Peter 4:10 says *"Each of you has been blessed with one of God's many wonderful gifts to be used in the service of others. So, use your gifts well."* Notice God gives you certain talents, abilities, personality, gifts -- the shape that He's given you -- and those gifts, those talents that you've been given are not for your benefit. They're for the benefit of other people. My gifts are for your benefit. Your gifts are for my benefit. You are to use those gifts in the service of other people. God has given you a special role in this world. He wants you to contribute with your life. God says, "I have given you these gifts and talents."

If you don't use your talents, you're going to lose your passion. God did not give you special abilities just to sit on them and do nothing about it. God wants you to use it, or you're going to lose it. Let me get specific. If you are stuck in a job that does not use your talents in any shape, form, nor fashion, you are inevitably going to lose your zeal and zest and passion in life. It's going to burn you out. Several years ago, I heard Rick Warren of Saddleback Ministries preach a sermon on having a passion for God. He mentioned that 70% of all Americans are in a job that does not use their talents. I remember thinking to myself; it is so easy to get caught up in making a living that you forget to live your lives. That particularly hit home with me because at the time I was working overtime on two jobs while at the same time not investing enough time in the area I was most passionate in. God did not give you talents and then say, "Don't use them. Just go make some money."

THERE IS SOMETHING IN LIFE THAT IS MORE IMPORTANT THAN MONEY.

That is using what God gave you. God is grieved when He looks and sees you in a job that's not using your talents. He's going, "What do you think I gave you your talents for? Just to sit on them?" No. If you do that, you're going to lose your passion. The reality is you're never going to find a job that uses 100% of your talent. You're never going to find a job that is

100% fulfilling. Why? Because God never meant for you to find 100% fulfillment through your job. *Your life is more than your job.*

If there is one thing that has drawn people to The Awakening Prayer Call or LaTrice Ryan Ministries, it was probably the passion I have for ministry. Not just passion for preaching, but being passionate about seeing the lives of God's people change for the better. If that means praying for an hour, until my hair is wringing wet, until my clothes are drenched in sweat, or until the young man who was wrestling with giving his life to Jesus finally accepts the call of salvation. Then it was worth it.

"It's not the size of the dog in the fight; It's the size of the fight in the dog."

Determination, passion, and commitment go hand in hand. There will be inevitable setbacks along the way to achieving success, and without the determination to overcome these roadblocks, commitment begins to waver. We must face obstacles with resiliency and courage. This involves learning to solve problem and take the necessary steps to work past barriers. Instead of viewing change and unexpected outcomes as problems we can begin to see them as challenges. We can start to feel invigorated and energized by the chance to rise to the occasion. Being determined means we accept and perceive these challenges as a part of the journey toward the larger accomplishment we are committed to.

When I was in the fourth grade, I learned a poem by Dr. Herbert W. Brewster entitled, "I'm Determined to Be Somebody Someday." The first stanza of the poem is this:

"The present conditions and dark circumstance May make it appear that I have not a chance. The odds may be against me; this fact I admit. I haven't much to boast of, just a little faith and grit. In spite of the things that stand in my way, I'M DETERMINED TO BE SOMEBODY SOMEDAY!"

Whether your passion is for protecting the environment, baking cookies, singing, teaching, or preaching, pursuing it will definitely give you opportunities to benefit other people by sharing your creations or knowledge. It may also open up possibilities for following your life passion as a job. My passion for as long as I can remember is inspiring others to love life and to feel good about themselves. That is something that comes natural to me, and I enjoy it to the fullest. For me, when I see a person who may be down or depressed and God uses me to pray for them or even say or do something that literally revives them… That is a feeling that I cannot explain. Giving another person life gives me life. Time is nearly nonexistent because I love inspiring others. That is something I am passionate about. You can feel the passion through a YouTube video or FaceBook live. Many things can be duplicated or even fabricated; however, it is difficult to produce in an area that you lack passion.

It takes courage to face the uncertainty, fear, and discomfort of branching out of the ordinary and into the extraordinary. Making a definite decision to be committed means you must take action. This means potential excuses must be accounted for ahead of time, and there can be no more waiting for the perfect moment. Keep going until it's done!

So, find your life passion, and go for it with your whole heart. Time spent doing what you love will never be time wasted.

CHAPTER 4

TAKE YOUR FIRST STEP

Job 8:7 "Though your beginning was small, yet your latter end would increase abundantly." NKJV

"I don't want to do it because it will be small." "I'm too little" "I don't have enough of…" "I'm too young." "We are not big enough" "My church is too small" "My business is too small" "Our budget is small."

This is one of my favorite chapters of the book. I like to call this chapter "The Pep Talk." When you hear the term "pep talk," you might immediately think of a sports movie with a head coach in a locker room pushing his team to be their best. The most powerful scenes in movies are the ones when the coach offers the team words of wisdom and motivation. He encourages them to get excited about the game and helps them dismiss any self-doubt they have about what they are getting ready to face. When the team gets on the field, there is nothing they can't accomplish. Wouldn't it be wonderful to have your own coach cheering you on and motivating you right when you need it most? Well, you do have a coach- it's you!

If there is anyone in the bible whom I can relate to most, it's probably King David. David is the youngest son of his father, Jesse. The Lord told the prophet Samuel to go down to Jesse's house to anoint the next king because the next king was one of Jesse's sons. Jesse presented his older sons before Samuel; Samuel looked at each of Jesse's sons, but God had not chosen either of them. Samuel then asks Jesse, "Do you have any more children?" Jesse says, "Yes, but he's outside tending to the sheep." David was not even considered a candidate to be king. I'm sure his father loved him, but he never saw David's true potential. *Side note: Just because others don't see your potential; it doesn't mean that it's not there.*

God had forewarned Samuel in 1 Samuel 16:7, "But the Lord said to Samuel, "Do not look at his appearance or at his physical stature, because I have refused him. For the Lord does not see as man sees; [a] for man looks at the outward appearance, but the Lord looks at the heart." David didn't look kingly; he had no formal training that would suggest maybe one day he'd be king. He was underrated, overlook, yet he was the one God chose. That was a little history of David. Back to 1 Samuel 30, David and his men suffered a surprise attack at the hands of the Amalekites. The Amalekites attacked the city, destroyed the city, and captured the women and children. All of David's men were distraught, and David's soldiers wanted to kill him. If there was ever a day David needed an encourager, it was this day. David needed a locker room at halftime moment. David needed someone to coach him from defeat back to victory. Now David had several options which would have been justifiable in this case. He could have wallowed in his defeat. He could have had survivor's remorse - a mental condition that occurs when a person believes they had done something wrong by surviving a traumatic event when others did not. When no one was available to encourage him, the bible says in 1 Samuel 30:6, "And David was greatly distressed; for the people spoke of stoning him, because the soul of all the people was grieved, every man for his sons and for his daughters: but David encouraged himself in the Lord his God."

David began to encourage himself. When you are faced with a hardship and need a pep talk, and no one is available, all hope is not lost. David encouraged himself. David gave himself the pep talk that he needed when he needed it most. There are moments in life when you have to be your biggest cheerleader.

That is not arrogance nor is it being conceited. Let me say this; when a person views your confidence as arrogance, it's probably because they are insecure with themselves. (I will deal more with confidence in my upcoming book *It's Your Crown: ROCK IT)*

The next time you need a pep talk, look in the mirror and speak these words over your life: *"Today, I will enter into a competition with myself to become the most extraordinary person I can be! No doubts or fears will be able to stop me from reaching my dreams because I am resilient and strong. I will not shrink my dreams to make them more doable. Instead, I will supersize myself! I will work hard today to silence all doubt. If anyone doubts how far I can go, I will go so far that I just can't hear there negativity anymore! I can push past all of their expectations, including my own. The most admired and successful people in the world were not free of insecurity or error or self-doubt; they just kept showing up and trying, no matter how many times it took until they got what they wanted. My dreams are just around the corner – let's go get them!"*

There will be days that you are mentally exhausted and feel like nothing can go right. No matter how hard you try at something, it just doesn't seem to work. Use this pep talk to help get you back on track. *Today, I will celebrate the amount of effort I have put in instead of focusing on the outcome. Every expert started out as a beginner, and that doesn't exclude me! With effort, resilience, and patience I will be able to accomplish anything I set my mind to. I will banish all discouragement and negative thoughts from my mind. There is no gain without a little pain! Practice is how you learn, and I will continue to practice no matter how frustrated I may feel. I can do it because I believe in myself*

Everyone goes through tough times in life. It's okay to struggle. Use this pep talk to get through some of the hardest of days: *Today, I will remember that I am much stronger than I think, braver than I believe and smarter than I think. Despite what life has thrown at me, I will not back down. I will continue to push forward and become a stronger person because of this! I have survived 100 percent of my worst days in life, so I just need to keep going. There is always light at the end of the tunnel. It's okay to be sad and frustrated, but I will continue to walk through life. I will be strong for those who need me, and I will be a superhero for myself. I will not let this break me.*

We go through life having to deal with people who are mean, cruel and downright toxic to be around. These people can very easily bring you down, but only if you let them. Use this pep talk when you are faced with a toxic relationship in your life: *Today, I will not forget how much I am worth, and I will not let someone else tell me otherwise. This person who is trying to drag me down is only doing so because they are beneath me. I am better than that, and I will not stoop to their level. I will not feed into their self-hate and anger. I am a fine piece of China, and I refuse to let anyone treat me like a paper plate. I will stand up for myself when necessary and walk away from situations that hurt me – because I know I am worth it! I can face this person with dignity and strength.*

You don't need an active football coach to get a great pep talk – you can do it yourself! These pep talks will help you become your own best coach. Take the time each day to identify what you are struggling in and push yourself to get past your inner doubt. A simple pep talk will make all the difference! Below are quick and easy pep talks. Write them on post-it notes. Place them in areas of your home, on your computer desk in your office, or any area that you frequent, it could be on the steering wheel of the car or even on the refrigerator.

Check out these quick pep talks. They are sure to get you started on conquering your goals.

- The hardest step is the first one.

- It's also the smallest, and often the simplest.

- Momentum is more powerful than we realize. But the snowball won't roll unless you give the first push.

- It's hard to start, but it's even harder to stop once we've started.

- Start something small every day. Watch them pile up.

- Choosing not to start is choosing to fail.

- Find a reason that makes it worth it.

- What will happen if you don't begin? What might you miss?

- Make the first step so small it'd be impossible not to take.

- The only thing standing between dreaming and beginning is you.

- Start first. Think later.

- If you don't start, nothing else matters.

- Most of the fear comes from anticipating the start.

- Most of the fear disappears once you begin.

- Don't leave the sight of an idea without doing one thing to get it closer to reality.

- Say no to something that doesn't matter, so you can start one thing that does.

- Possibility cannot live until you begin.

- If you don't start, you can't finish.

- Starting is what builds a bridge, creates a business, loses 100 pounds, writes a best-seller. Starting does it all.

- Starting is what changes the world. It's the only thing that ever has.

- Everything starts by starting. When is now a good time?

- It all comes back to that first step.

- It is our responsibility to take it. To see what's possible when we decide to stop dreaming and start doing.

- The world tries to talk ourselves out of it. Stop listening.

Starting can be anything. For me, it was writing this book. Do you know how many prophecies I have received concerning me writing a book? Do you know how many people have asked, "When is the book being released?" I have been writing a book for over ten years. I will start and stop. I'll start, lose focus, and stop. I purchased all of the book writing software. I don't know where 90% of it is today.

I said to myself, "No one would buy it?" "What do I have to say?" "How can I write a book?" It doesn't matter if it's making a phone call, scheduling a meeting, sketching a design, running a mile or walking around the block, reading the first page or writing the first sentence. Whether it's saying "yes" or saying "I quit." Take five minutes to start something right now. Imagine what it could become. The world will thank you and so will you. This chapter is a Pep Rally. Imagine it's the most anticipated game of the season. It's Homecoming Weekend, and your team is facing its biggest rival. This is the moment where our focus is on taking action. Our focus is getting started not passively reading. Start small. Start now. No matter what or how - Get Started!

NO MORE EXCUSES

In any occupation, there are elements that are not as "fun" as other elements of that occupation. As a result, many people will often slow themselves down in an effort to "avoid" those boring or tedious elements that they don't like doing as much as the fun aspects of their job or occupation.

In truth, those efforts to make excuses, and just avoid certain aspects of an occupation or task just lead to people taking longer to complete work they could do much quicker, leading to them getting less done than they could within a set amount of time. Additionally, it forces them to work harder, take more time away from other activities they'd rather be doing and can lead them to do poorer-quality work because they have to work faster to make up for the time they lost by procrastinating and making excuses. Due to the fact they are working faster, they're more prone to making mistakes and not thinking clearly when doing important tasks.

CHAPTER 5

FOCUS!

"Whenever you want to achieve something, keep your eyes open, concentrate and make sure you know exactly what it is you want. No one can hit their target with their eyes closed."
Paulo Coelho

I f you cannot remain focused on your goals, you will lose momentum and fail to make the progress you desire. This soon leads to a loss of confidence and motivation. You may blame distractions such as work, family, or technology and say that's the reason why you have a hard time concentrating on your goals. I mean, these things will always be part of your life. If you are not achieving your goals and objectives, it is not good enough to blame outside factors. When you do so, you are actually giving away your personal power and denying that your success lies within your hands. What you need to do is find a way to manage these outside factors which allow you to stay focused on your goals and, maintain a healthy and balanced life.

The good news is that there are a few simple measures that you can take to help you stay focused on your goals. By implementing these steps from the moment, you set the goal; you will be more focused, more motivated and more determined. You will soon see that you are making progress towards your goals and so, you will be more likely to stick with it and see it through to completion.

Here are a few strategies to remain focused:

1. Narrow your list

I once considered myself a *Multi-Tasking Queen*. I would make dinner, help my children with homework, do laundry, write a sermon, pray for the nations, respond to emails, and update my social media accounts; LITERALLY ALL AT THE SAME TIME. In my mind, I was the bomb. I was Super Woman. I had an S on my chest with my glittery gold cape flying in the wind. I realize I was doing it all but surely was not doing anything well. Goals are great, but if you have too many of them, you will soon see that one goal is distracting you from working on another. Instead of trying to focus on too many goals, narrow it down to 1-3 major goals over a period of time. Burning the candle at both ends will eventually cause you to…BURN DOWN. Narrow your list to see progress. This ensures that you aren't spreading yourself too thin and, as a result, losing your motivation.

2. Break down each of your major goals

How do you eat a Whale? The answer – one bite at a time. The same strategy is critical for achieving your goals. Large goals can be very overwhelming. Remember my 40 by 40 weight loss goal? Due to my love of chocolate chip cookies and Chick Fil A French fries, it would be impossible for me to lose forty pounds in forty days. That would be a set up for failure. To make sure I remain focused, I gave myself one year to lose the weight by losing 3-4 pounds per month. You'll feel less overwhelmed when you break up a large goal into a series of smaller steps, each with specific, achievable tasks. Instead of focusing on the large goal, you focus on the smaller tasks which you need to complete. It will be less intimidating and, with each small task completed, you will receive a confidence boost as you realize that you are one step closer to your goal. This makes reaching your ultimate goal that much easier. As you accomplish each step, maintain your momentum and enthusiasm for achieving your goal by celebrating your success.

If you have a fitness goal, celebrate by buying clothes in a smaller size.

3. Have accountability partners

Accountability partners are NECESSARY. In the chapter "The Hardest Step is the First One" I mention there are times when you must be your own cheerleader and encourage yourself. There are moments when you have to be the voice of the coach in the locker room giving the team a pep talk. An accountability partner is not necessarily a cheerleader nor a coach; they are the ones in the trenches with you. You would not be reading this book if Kimberlyne Roundtree founder of Momentum Consulting was not one of my accountability partners. Kim bugged me to no end. I had very good excuse not to write - I travel extensively preaching the gospel, I'm a wife, mother, grandmother, community advocate, entrepreneur, daughter, friend, and a woman in my forties going through menopause. (The last reason is at the top of the list)... Thanks Kim for holding me to my goal.

It is perfectly fine to have different accountability partners for each goal. As long as the goal is not too personal or confidential in nature; telling people whom you trust about your goal will make you more accountable. You value friends and loved ones, and you value the respect that comes with their friendship. When you inform them of changes that you wish to make, you want to be seen to honor your word. Ideally, these people will encourage you when obstacles arise and celebrate your successes with you along the way. This support will help you to stay focused on your goals.

Here's a few things to look for when selecting an accountability partner:

- Someone who is interested in growth.

  They should be in interested in growth for themselves and seeing you grow.

  Do two walks together unless they have agreed to do so? Amos 3:3 (NIV)

- Someone who will be honest with you.

  Your accountability partner should be someone who would be honest with you in a spirit of love.

  What this adds up to, then, is this: no more lies, no more pretense. Tell your neighbor the truth. In Christ's body we're all connected to each other, after all. When you lie to others, you end up lying to yourself. Ephesians 4:25 (MSG)

- Someone who will remember to ask you.

  Create a check-in schedule - a daily text, weekly email, or meeting to discuss your progress.

  Therefore encourage one another and build up one another, just as you also are doing.

  1 Thessalonians 5:11 (NASB)

- Someone who will give you grace when you fail.

  There are times when you will fall or even fail. This is when your accountability partner gives you a hand up instead a kick when you're down.

  Brethren, if a man be overtaken in a fault, ye which are spiritual, restore such a one in the spirit of meekness; considering thyself, lest thou also be tempted. Galatians 6:1 (KJV)

4. Record, measure and document your progress

When you set a goal, one of the first things that you should do is decide how you will measure your progress. It is imperative that you know how you are progressing. Measure your goals by:

- Looking Backward, Not Forward.

Goal progress shouldn't be measured by where you aren't yet; it should be measured by where you are now compared to where you used to be.

- Keep and track your progress.

  Whether you keep up with your goals in an app, on your computer or a notepad, keep up with them. Use your past progress to reflect and plan future accomplishment.

- Look for patterns

  When you look back, check for any patterns in your actions. There are certain things that allow us to complete more goals, while other things end up making us less productive. Watch for both. In the words of psychologist Joshua P. Smith, "Patterns don't lie. People do."

5. Create a physical or digital vision board

To help you stay focused on your goals, you can create a visual reminder of why you created a particular goal in the first place. Take a poster board, bulletin board, or digital platform like Pinterest, and fill it with pictures, phrases, and other images that help you maintain your enthusiasm and focus. Vision Board gatherings are more than a Girls' Day outing, and it's definitely not a "ladies only" fad. I encourage couples to create a vision board for your relationship. Entrepreneurs create a vision board for your business. Vision Boards serve as both an enjoyable and effective method to stay focused on your goals.

"Successful people maintain a positive focus in life no matter what is going on around them. They stay focused on their past successes rather than their past failures, and on the next action steps they need to take to get them closer to the fulfillment of their goals rather than all the other distractions that life presents to them." Jack Canfield

With every single moment of our lives, we get to choose if we want to focus on the positive or negative things of our lives time. Focus not on your mistakes or failures, but concentrate on your past successes and draw strength from these experiences.

Why do racehorses wear blinders?

Horses have excellent peripheral vision. They can easily see what is around them or beside them. Horses sometimes need to be made to focus, and blinders keep the horse's eye focused on what is ahead, rather than what is at the side or behind. That is why racehorses are often given blinders – for the purpose of keeping them focused when racing around a racecourse. The jockey has a very small amount of control over the horse. If a horse decides to take a different route, it will simply take the jockey with it, so this can cause major problems. Some racehorses are fitted with blinders for their own safety, the jockey's safety, and to keep the horse focused forward.

It is so easy to become distracted with what's going on around you, beside you, or even behind you. Especially with people posting their lucrative job promotions, loving marriages, brilliant children, and international travels, you can end up making a disastrous move- Comparing yourself to others.

Comparing yourself to others' accomplishments is a losing battle. There is an infinite amount of people you could compare yourself and your accomplishments, but, inevitably, you'll always end up on the losing side of the equation. That's because there will always be someone who has done something that you wished you could also accomplish.

Comparison leads to a never ending downward spiral. Once you start comparing yourself to others, where do you draw the line? Do you compare only career-related achievements, such as job titles, compensation, perks, and benefits, or whether they have an office with a door or work in a cubicle? Do you compare personal accomplishments, such as who owns the most expensive car, the biggest house, got married first? Comparing yourself to others can be like falling down an endless rabbit hole. You can literally make yourself depressed by measuring path with others. You are unique, and not an exact duplicate of anyone else. Think about it. Even if you were the genetic twin to someone, you would have grown up with different experiences, different influences, different activities, ideas and thoughts. Your personalities wouldn't be the same. Your likes and dislikes wouldn't be the same. So why would your personal and career achievements be absolutely identical and accomplished at the same time? They wouldn't. Try to begin seeing everyone, even yourself, as unique individuals.

Find Your FLOW.

There is a difference between hustle and flow. Hustle is the work we do to try and keep up with the next person. When we are looking to compete with others and stay in the race. However, when you are in your FLOW, you are in competition with NO ONE. You no longer live hungry for people's perceptions nor approval. Making their happiness more important than my own. Instead what happens is you are free to follow you Inner GPS (your God Placement System) that I believe whispers to our soul to give us guidance along the way. I will tell you from my own personal experience: When you start following the little unction and urges that you get from your GPS, you begin to create a lane ALL your own. You tap into your own greatness, and you begin to find the level of success that is YOURS for the taking

One of the most effective ways to regain, maintain, and sustain your focus is through the word of God. Trust me. IT WORKS! Here are some of the affirmations I speak over my life daily:

- I can reach my goals and dreams! I call unto God, and He answers me, and shows me great and mighty things, which I know not. Jeremiah 33:3

- God is able to do exceeding abundantly above all that we ask or think, according to His power that works in us. Ephesians 3:20

- With God, my talents are being multiplied. I am blessed. I have unlimited potential. Deuteronomy 1:11

- Eye has not seen, nor ear heard, neither has it entered into my heart, the things which God has prepared for me. 1 Corinthians 2:9

- I have vision and purpose. I have faith that I can do anything that God has called me to do. Proverbs 29:18

- God is our all-knowing and unlimited God! He can see the end from the beginning. I pray for wisdom and direction in every area of my life. Isaiah 46:10

- Jesus is greater than any obstacle we face. Greater is He that is in me, than he that is in the world! 1 John 4:4

- As a child of the living God – we are made to be winners. We were born to succeed! We are made to be the head and not the tail; above only, and not beneath. We can have victory in every area of our life. Deuteronomy 28:13

- I can reach my goals and dreams! With God, all things are possible! Mark 10:27

- For the joy of the LORD is my strength (Neh 8:10)!

- I trust in the Lord with all my heart; and lean not unto my own understanding. In all my ways I acknowledge Him, and He shall direct my paths (Proverbs 3:5-6).

- Jesus keeps me in perfect peace, as my mind is stayed on Him: because I trust in Him (Isaiah 26:3).

- I wait upon the Lord, and He renews my strength; I mount up with wings as eagles, I run, and am not weary; I walk, and am not faint (Isaiah 40:31).

- My delight is in the law of the Lord, and in His law do I meditate day and night. And I shall be like a tree planted by the rivers of water, that brings forth his fruit in his season, my leaf also shall not wither, and whatever I do, shall prosper (Psalms 1:2-3).

CHAPTER 6
YOU ARE A FINISHER

John 4:34: "Jesus said to them, 'My food is to do the will of him who sent me and to accomplish his work.'"

John 17:4: "I glorified you on earth, having accomplished the work that you gave me to do."

God gave Jesus work. Not to merely try – but to accomplish. To finish. Jesus was a finisher.

Willpower is what helps you finish! It is the inner strength and the inner engine that moves towards success and accomplishment. It's the might that pushes into action in each area of life.

Willpower is among the most of import and worthy inner powers, and its lack or presence determines whether you'll fail or achieve your wants and aspirations and accomplish success. It is mistakenly considered as a quality belonging only to extremely successful individuals, who depend upon strength and power to accomplish their goals. The reality is that it may be developed by everybody, and it's crucial, useful and desirable in the little affairs of life, as it's in the accomplishment of major goals.

If you feel too lazy, developing your inner strength will help you to overpower this laziness. If you commonly possess low self-esteem, feel powerless and vulnerable or lack self-control, fortifying this power will help you.

Willpower, which is the inner strength to finish something, evidence as the power to command unnecessary and disadvantageous impulses. It likewise manifests as the power to decide, abide by this decision, and follow it with perseverance till its successful achievement. This power gives you the bravery and strength to endure and overpower inner and outer resistance, troubles and hardships.

There are several who lack the inner strength to state "no." Other people find it hard to follow and assert their ideas and notions. A few are afraid to take action and make changes, or they lack resolution and the doggedness to go on with their plans to the end. A secure power of the will may alter all this.

It's the right and privilege of everybody to formulate this power. Everybody may develop it to a greater or smaller extent, depending upon the desire, serious-mindedness, ambition and time devoted to formulating and fortifying this inner strength.

You don't require ultraordinary powers to formulate it. You don't have to sleep on a bed of nails, fast or stand on one foot for days.

Developing inner power is a gradual process that anybody may undertake. A few will be able to accomplish higher levels of power, while other people will accomplish different degrees of development, but the way is open to all.

You'll have to give up a few unneeded and harmful pleasures and alter a few unhealthy habits, but this is for a higher good. You give up something adverse or useless, in order to acquire strength and power that will help you in each area of your life. As a matter of fact, the whole procedure may be turned into an absorbing, gratifying and interesting challenge.

Training and exercising your willpower will fill you with strength, bravery, and self-assertiveness. As your power develops, it will be simpler for you to get rid of habits and attitudes that stand in your way to a more beneficial life. You'll acquire inner strength that will help you at your occupation and home, in your relationships, with conducting your tasks and achieving your aspirations.

How many times have you wished you had more inner strength, self-control or self-discipline?

How many times did you lack adequate doggedness and inner stamina to follow your choices and plans?

Do you look up to and respect strong people, who have overpowered obstacles and troubles and reached far, because of the inner strength they had?

Most individuals are not born with inner strength, but it may be developed like any other skill.

Inner strength consists of willpower, self-discipline, self-control, doggedness, detachment, the power to concentrate and peace of mind. These skills are crucial and essential tools for success in all areas of life. They may be learned and developed like any other skill, yet, despite this, only few take any steps to develop and fortify them in an orderly way.

Here are a few drills to beef up your willpower in ordinary day-to-day actions:

➢ Don't watch the news for a couple of days.

➤ From time to time, drink your tea without sugar.

➤ Climb up the stairs rather than taking the elevator.

➤ Park your car a little further away from your destination, so that you have to walk.

➤ Now and then, choose not to watch one of your favorite television shows.

➤ Read a book that's useful and enlightening, but which you find tedious.

These are only a couple of illustrations to show you how you are able to formulate your inner strength. By rehearsing these or like exercises, you acquire inner power, which you are able to utilize when you're in need of it. By rehearsing them, you formulate your inner muscles, just like lifting weights develops your physical muscles. This helps you finish.

FOR THE WIN

The phrase "For the Win" probably most recognized from the game show Hollywood Squares where the result of the player's response is expected to win the game. The phrase is often said in victory, but you can also say it while you're very near to victory, or even just working toward your goal. In other words, it's something of a modern-day rallying cry - it says my next move is not to tie the game, but to win the game.

"The term 'Winning' may sound phony to you. Too materialistic. Too full of A's, or luck, or odds, or muscle-bound athletes. True winning, however, is no more than one's own personal pursuit of individual excellence. You don't have to knock other people down or gain at the expense of others. 'Winning' is taking the talent and potential you were born with, and have since developed, and using it fully toward a goal or purpose that makes you happy." Dennis Waitley, author of The Psychology of Winning.

As you can clearly see from the quote above "winners" and "losers" are not about competition. There is not a line separating the 1% as "winners" from the rest of us. Winning is not about materialism, or simply about sport. It is about finding your success in life, whatever that may be. It may be about finding happiness. It may be about achieving a peaceful mind. It is about being a success in the life you desire and working to achieve all your goals. If there is anything, I have learned while writing this book and even in life itself - habits are everything. There is an old saying that says, "You will play how you've practiced." If you want to perform strongly in any area (from sports to business to ministry), you can't slack off in your practice, because what you do most of the time is what you get used to.

"Practice doesn't make perfect. Perfect practice makes perfect." Vince Lombardi

Winning, according to Waitley is not about demolishing your competition. It is simply about developing a positive, growth mindset and building those winning habits. One clear distinction Waitley makes between life's winners, and losers are that winners build good habits that help them succeed while losers retain all their bad habits and are content to live a life with fear and regret. Winners practice daily habits that we should also practice if we plan to Go for The Win:

Unleash the power of self-determination

The word "determination" has multiple meanings depending on the context of its usage. One definition says: "The quality of being determined to do or achieve something."

In simpler terms, it means how much of yourself you will put into making a goal a reality. You need to feel invested in the things you do. Make the decision to be determined. A strong, specific decision needs to be made so as to become more determined in anything. This decision indicates your direction. It shows you how to move forward even when you begin to encounter challenges on your path. This decision is set in stone, motivates you through hard times and keeps you focused during easy times. As such, determination begins by deciding what you want and sticking to your decision no matter what.

Embrace your imperfections

No one is perfect. We all have our flaws and shortcomings. Being a winner is not about being perfect and always succeeding regardless of the odds. It is about knowing your weaknesses and planning for them. To be a winner you may need to outsource or delegate tasks that are difficult for you, and that's ok. I am surrounded by people who are smarter than me. My team consists of people who can perform better in the areas that I am weak in. You may need to delegate a lot of extra time for tasks that others can do quickly. Focusing on your core genius. It is all about this understanding of yourself. Embracing your imperfections will allow you to empathize with others. If you understand how those around you feel, and can feel their situations and pain, it gives you a broad base of understanding.

This understanding can even lead to being more adaptable and ready for a change. When you increase your adaptability, the odd things that always "pop up" that might cause the goals of others to fail will never derail you from success. Being adaptable means, you will roll with the punches and simply recalibrate your plans to include the new changed situation.

Positive Self-Esteem

It is important to have a healthy self-esteem and self-confidence to be a winner. I consider my husband Derek to be one of the most confident men I know. My position as a ministry leader does not intimidate him. Reason being, he is confident in himself and his gifting in our ministry. I am the preacher and Derek is my priest. Together we are a winning combination because where I am weak, he is strong and vice versa. Can I be honest with you? My husband is the mastermind behind LaTrice Ryan Ministries and Ryan Enterprises. You do not need to have the spotlight, be the front man, or be an extrovert to have a healthy self-esteem and self-confidence. You simply have to have faith in yourself.

Self-Discipline

No one likes to hear that success is going to take a lot of work. Many people want easy answers and instant results these days. They want the shortcuts that will get them around the hard, messy, "work" part of the equation. Sorry to say, there are no overnight successes. To achieve your goals, you will need to build the hard habits. You will need the self-discipline to keep them going… and the self-discipline to start them once again if you happen to fail the first time.

Put Fear in Its Place - Don't Let Fear Stop You

"You miss 100% of the shots you don't take."- Wayne Gretzky

In other words, you can't succeed unless you try and that means you have to take action. Taking that first step is sometimes the hardest part. It's easy to picture ourselves being successful, but it's a whole other thing to take physical steps to attain and accomplish our goals and dreams. Fear, insecurity, and inadequacy often get in the way, but that's not something we should be surprised by – actually, Jesus warned us about this problem over 2,000 years ago: "I have told you these things, so that in me you may have peace. In this world you will have trouble. But take heart! I have overcome the world." -John 16:33-

Nike said it best – it's not until we set aside our fears, take heart and JUST DO IT that anything happens! Don't sit by and let another day come and go without taking your shots.

Here's why you should DO IT NOW:

The benefit usually outweighs the risk- If you take the shot and make it, you feel a huge sense of accomplishment. If you miss, you have the joy of knowing you at least tried. Believe me, people have all sorts of ideas, plans, and dreams but will allow their fear of failure – or their fear of success - to stop them from even trying. It may have something to do with worrying about what other people will think or it may have to do with a lack of confidence. Either way, taking the shot is a far better choice than not. Maybe you'll nail it? Maybe you make some gains? Anything can happen when you try. On the flip side don't take the shot and you are sure to stay right where you are for the rest of your life. *Take the shot*.

Even if you miss, you won't regret it- I have ministered to countless of people, I find that it isn't the failures or mistakes that get people down and depressed. No, it is the shot and chance they never even took that creates the most lasting damage – all the things they never even tried to do. When it is all said and done, you don't want to be the one sitting there thinking about all the shots you never even took in life – all the opportunities you weren't open to. Regret is a hard thing to live with. It is harder than failure.

"Some people want it to happen, some wish it would happen, others make it happen"-Michael Jordan

You learn what you are made of- Taking the shot builds confidence, and the more shots you take and miss, the more powerful you become because you just stop being afraid of failure. You become free of fear (fear keeps people in bondage) and learn that you actually can and do just go on. You become more courageous, more determined, more committed – and you learn how to get it right or whether or not you should do something different. Success breeds success. Trying breeds success. And failure – yes failure – breeds success (when you try something and then learn from it). You can make choices from facts and effort instead of something you never experienced. And baby, when you take that shot and actually make it, there is just no better feeling than that! I have taken so many shots in my life. I have actually missed far more shots than I have made, but when I make the shot – WOW! Nothing feels so good as matching hard effort, sweat, and tears with the desired outcome. It is an amazing feeling and experience indeed, and it builds confidence! But guess what? You only get to know that joy if you actually take the shot. There were things you didn't know you could do until you did it.

You become an inspiration to others- We all want to be around other people who are doing great things and going places. We want to learn, to grow and to be challenged and excited by the possibility of a better tomorrow. Think about how you feel when you are engaged in dialogue with someone who is excited about a future prospect, sharing his/her goals and dreams with you or starting a new project, a new job, a new family. Now think about talking with that person after he/she has turned that prospect into reality and/or accomplished the goals and dreams! Imagine you with all of the obstacles in your way, but you still tried when quitting was an easier and quicker option. Imagine how many people who will believe God for greater simply because you took the shot. Your testimony will convince the world that Jesus is real. God wants to use your life as a witness to His unlimited power.

Listen, don't leave anything on the table. There will always be risks involved when you go for it. One of my favorite scriptures is 1 John 4:4 *"You, dear children, are from God and have overcome them, because the one who is in you is greater than the one who is in the world."* This scripture reminds us no matter the obstacles surrounding you, no matter the fear that's staring you eye to eye; we have already overcome them because of the power of God that lies within us!

Today is the day to TAKE THE SHOT. No more saying, "I'll do it later" News flash, the word "later" ALMOST ALWAYS turns into another word ... NEVER.

Today is the day that we stop shifting the blame to haters, doubters, naysayers. Instead of blaming them, use them as ammunition to get up and nail our goals.

The only thing keeping you from taking the shot is you. Nothing else! It only takes one moment to make a decision. One moment to say no and one moment to say yes. One moment to decide to settle for mediocrity and one moment to strive for greatness. One moment to remove yourself from toxic nonproductive relationships and environments. One moment to be strong.

Many people try new ideas, and when they don't go well for them, they give up and feel like failures. Others, after trying new ideas and failing refuse to give up and continue to try and many of them succeed, and those who don't just enjoy the experience and turn their hands to something else.

Why do some people choose to make the most of the experience no matter what the result may be and others rate it a failure if things don't go well? The answer is an optimistic attitude to every experience in life. Successes are achievements enjoyed today and failures are learning tools for future experiences. There are no failures; they are simply steps towards future successes.

Learning to laugh at our mistakes and to dream big dreams are two very important characteristics that optimists develop that enable them to look at something that some may call as a failure as a learning opportunity. When we take our selves too seriously, we are more likely to think of our failures as permanent, and they often attack our sense of self worth. When we can focus on our other successes and see this as a setback that we can laugh at and continue to dream of success next time we maintain our optimism.

So how do we deal with failure so we can see it as a learning tool for the future?

1. Challenge what you think of success and failure. It's our perception of them that makes us see failure as negative and success as positive. Failure is simply part of the journey to success, the ultimate destination.

2. When you feel a failure because of a poor result or outcome, set yourself goals immediately, deciding how to continue your journey to success. The old, but familiar saying of "climb back on your horse immediately after you fall off" is based on this concept.

3. Look at a failure from the perspective of the big picture, not the small picture. You may have not achieved the outcome you wanted, but you did achieve. Make a list of all the things you learned and gained from experience and celebrate those things. They are achievements, it is not one complete failure, but many small achievements and they deserve to be celebrated.

Failure is about opportunity, and embracing failure as opportunity helps to eliminate failure from your vocabulary helping you to stay optimistic and find success in everything you do.

Conquering Your Fear of Failure

Some people find it hard to accept failure. When you grow up in an environment where perfectionism is a must and failure is unacceptable, you naturally grow up being afraid of failure. When you've experienced adverse effects of previous failures, you acquire the fear of failing again. You get butterflies in your stomach every time you think about disappointing the people you love. You'd hate for them to be humiliated because of your failure so you try to avoid doing anything that can cause you, and them, to lose face in front of other people.

A favorite excuse of people who fear failure is the saying "better safe than sorry." When you have an irrational fear of failing, you don't give yourself the chance to succeed. You'd rather stay "safe" in your comfort zone. You don't challenge yourself. You're too afraid to try anything new. Or if you do try, you quit far too early because you doubted yourself and didn't think you'd ever succeed. Having this mindset is a huge barrier to finishing anything. Self-growth is at the bottom of your priorities.

In June of 2017, we held our Fifth Annual Unshakable Faith Weekend in Atlanta, Georgia. We have hosted the conference in my hometown for four consecutive years. Well for the fifth year we ventured to push our limits. God gave us the vision to host the conference, not only in a different city and state but in a different time zone. We held the luncheon at a hotel that I had never visited. We did not have the workforce, budget, nor resources to pull off a conference of this magnitude. I had a plethora of emotions ranging from sheer exuberance to downright nail-biting anxiety. I did not know if anyone would attend. I did not know if it would succeed, the only thing I knew is that I would try.

May I be honest with you? I am not a pastor of a mega church. I do not have a worldwide ministry with millions of followers. YET... There are more people who have never heard of LaTrice Ryan Ministries than there are of people who have heard of us. This is why humility is essential for expansion. Sometimes we can be a celebrity in our neighborhood. All you have to do is go around the corner, and no one even knows your name. The only name we want to make famous in LaTrice Ryan Ministries is the name of Jesus.

We were virtually unknown in a city of which hosts booming influential conferences every day. We were a small fish in a big pond serving the God who created both the fish and the pond. We had every reason to keep the conference in a familiar place, but keeping a God-inspired vision boxed in and buried brought no glory to GOD! We challenged our thinking. We challenged our capacity. We challenged our limits. As a result, Unshakable Faith 2017 was the most successful conference to date. We had over 1200 attendees at the revival and over 500 luncheon attendees. We did not go in the red logistically. A little amount in the hands of God becomes MAJOR DEAL. Everything God has given us to do we never had the money to do it. PLEASE do not allow money to be the reason you do not finish what God told you to do.

Risks are inherent when taking on new challenges. When you don't take risks, you avoid failing. But smart and well-disciplined people know that not all risk is bad. In fact, risk can be mitigated by studying and calculating the odds of success.

When setting yourself up to reach a new goal, you try to learn all the details about what you hope to do so you know if your goal is feasible and achievable.

Being meticulous with your goal planning is important to minimize risk and failure. If you visualize the process as I mentioned earlier in this book, then you should be able to overcome your fear of failure. You will know the exact steps you need to take to realize your goal, and you're essentially leaving very little to chance.

Overcoming Your Fear Of Success? Is That a Thing?

Most people can easily understand or relate to fearing failure. Fearing success is another matter altogether and is less easily understood by many because its symptoms can easily be mistaken for insecurity and procrastination. In this section, I'll go through the main symptoms that characterize this kind of fear.

The first sign is you feel like you don't deserve success or you feel unworthy. You're stifling your growth and even greater success because you feel like a fraud. You think someone else deserves your success more than you do because you've been blessed with resources that other people have to work hard to get. You think this gives you an unfair head start, and as such, don't deserve success.

The second sign of fearing of success is when you fear other people's expectations of you. You're afraid they'll expect something from you that you can't possibly deliver. Being successful and being in the spotlight can bring about people who expect you to be a constant achiever. For example, you're afraid that if you become a successful writer, people will expect you to write bestselling novels all the time with captivating storylines and intricate plot twists. You're afraid that people will hate you and stop reading your books if you publish a less than stellar novel. So because of your fear, you just continue writing your awesome stories on your computer, with no plans of ever publishing it and sharing it with the world.

The third sign is you're afraid of being isolated. You don't want people to put you on a pedestal because you're not that kind of person. You still want to have down time with your friends even after you're successful, but you're afraid they're going to keep you at arm's reach, and you don't want that. You might also have friends who might be jealous of your success and don't want to have anything to do with you any more simply because they're insecure about their lack of success.

The fourth sign is you're afraid of turning into someone you don't like. You see it all the time happening before our very eyes. You're afraid of turning into a monster who thinks he can buy everything and everyone with money. You don't want to be one of them, so you don't pursue your dreams and instead continue hiding in your shell. Having an increase financially does not bring out the worst in you, it reveals what is already in you. If you have an extra $20 from your paycheck after paying all of your bills, saving, and tithing; and the first thing you buy with the extra dollars is an ice cream cone. The moment you come into some serious money, you may buy an ice cream shop. Because money does not bring out the worst in you, it simply reveals what was always there.

Lastly, you might be afraid of change; you might be afraid of the unknown that success will inevitably bring. You don't want to upset your routines and your current setup at home. You read bedtime stories to your kids now. If you're successful, you'll be so busy with work and managing people and clients that you won't have time for your family and they'll end up hating you for it.

If you really want to pursue success in life, you're going to need self-discipline and self-control to keep on going after what you want. You're going to have to fight against your fear of success because if you don't, then you're not going to get very far in life.

Stop Sabotaging Yourself

The first step to curing your self-sabotaging tendencies is to acknowledge that you have a problem. You have to recognize that you have a very real fear of failure and success because if you don't own up to it, you're not going to find the cure for your 'condition.'

If you think hiding behind a smiling mask will hide your fears, you're wrong. You can possibly attain short-term success behind a mask but doing so will take enormous amounts of energy and will eventually sap you of strength. Being true to yourself and acknowledging you have issues is the only way you can stop sabotaging yourself.

Also, try being an optimist. When your fears and your self-doubt starts weighing you down, look beyond the negativity and try to look at the other, more positive side of things. When you get to thinking there's no way you can possibly succeed, snap yourself out of it because you know that is not true. Many people have successfully overcome the odds stacked against them and have gone on to live fulfilling lives.

Know that with self-discipline and self-control, you can overcome your fears and find success in almost anything you put your mind to. Success doesn't happen overnight. You have to put in the time - and the work - to succeed in anything in life. Stop sabotaging your efforts at disciplining yourself!

Affirmations

Fear is an Illusion

Fear is an illusion in the mind, and I know I can overcome it. I refuse to listen to the inner voice that tells me to be afraid.

Instead of allowing my fears to be in charge, I control my body and mind.

I have the power to stop fear before it takes over. I put together a list of all of my fears so I can be on the lookout for them and stop them in their tracks. I can let go of my fears. My mind is strong and able to see beyond a moment of fear. I recognize my talents and pursue my dreams regardless of any fears that may arise.

I can avoid panic because I know I am strong and powerful.

My mind is open to the truth about self-imposed limits. Fear is one of these limits, but I am stronger than the illusion. I leave fears behind and let my creativity blossom. I avoid creating boundaries for my spirit.

My mind is a unique vessel that functions without fear.

Today, I am free. Free to go after my dreams. Free from the illusion that tries to make me afraid. And free to create the life I desire.

Finish What You Started

When it comes to completing a job, task, or project, have you ever choked under the pressure and wondered if you would finish? If this has happened to you, you might have ended up feeling guilty and profoundly disappointed in your own abilities.

Even though your desire for an end result is high, the difficulty level or time required to complete the task could make you want to give up.

Where do you stand when it comes to persevering until a job is complete? How can you persist when you're challenged in meeting your goals?

If you struggle to complete what you start, these strategies are for you:

1. **Be consistent.** Sometimes, it feels like you'll never get there. When you feel that way, remind yourself you must simply keep on keeping on. If you stay with working consistently toward your goal, chances are good you'll eventually accomplish it.

2. **Notice what you've done so far.** *When you can see some fruits of your labors, you'll get another burst of motivation to keep going.* Maybe you completed 10% of the project last week. That's 10% less than you have to do to finish. Have an acute awareness of what you've already completed as well as what you have left to do.

3. **Maintain a positive outlook.** Whenever you stay focused on the positive, it just makes it easier to continue plodding forward. ***Being positive is a choice, so take advantage of it.*** Accentuate the positive.

4. **Avoid under-estimating what it will take to finish.** We've all had the experience of thinking we know how long we will spend to complete a particular task, only to find it takes much longer. If you must make a ball-park guess as to how much time you'll need, it's better to over-estimate.

5. **Make a personal vow to finish what you've started.** Staying conscious of what you want to do and why you want to do it and then vowing to finish will serve as motivation to help you keep your nose to the grindstone. Promise yourself you'll persist until you prevail. Then do it.

6. **Recognize when you must tweak your results.** There may be times when you wish to slightly alter your end goal. After all, situations and people change. ***Particularly for long-term projects and goals, stay focused so that you'll identify when it's time to make alterations.***

- If what you want hasn't changed, it's okay. Just revisit the goal, tweak it, and keep moving forward.

FINISHING can be a challenge, but it's well worth it. Be consistent and take note of what you've accomplished. Stay as positive. Vow to finish and stay aware of what you're doing so you can adjust your goal if you need to.

Finally, persist until you finish!

Made in the USA
Columbia, SC
20 April 2018